LOOK AHEAD

a guide to working in...

Information Technology

Deborah Fortune

INFORMATION TECHNOLOGY

www.heinemann.co.uk
Visit our website to find out more information about **Heinemann Library** books.

To order:
☎ Phone 44 (0) 1865 888066
▤ Send a fax to 44 (0) 1865 314091
▭ Visit the Heinemann Bookshop at www.heinemann.co.uk to browse our catalogue and order online.

First published in Great Britain by Heinemann Library,
Halley Court, Jordan Hill, Oxford OX2 8EJ,
a division of Reed Educational and Professional Publishing Ltd.
Heinemann is a registered trademark of Reed Educational & Professional Publishing Ltd.

OXFORD MELBOURNE AUCKLAND
JOHANNESBURG BLANTYRE GABORONE
IBADAN PORTSMOUTH NH (USA) CHICAGO

Designed by Ambassador Design Ltd, Bristol.
Originated by Ambassador Litho, Bristol.
Printed in Hong Kong/China

ISBN 0 431 09483 7
04 03 02 01 00
10 9 8 7 6 5 4 3 2 1

British Library Cataloguing in Publication Data
Fortune, Deborah
   A guide to working in IT – (Look ahead)
   1. Information technology – vocational guidance – Great Britain
   I. Title II.IT
   004'.02341

Acknowledgements
The Publishers would like to thank the following for permission to reproduce photographs:
Ace Photo Agency/SMP Assocs, p. 18; Action Plus, p. 39; Gareth Boden, pp. 43, 54; Images Colour Library, p. 14; Pictor International, pp. 7, 17, 28; Post Studies, p. 35; Powerstock Zefa, pp. 10, 20, 25; Stock Market, p. 32; Stone, pp. 26, 37, 46, /Bruce Ayres p. 23; Telegraph Colour Library/Samuel Ashfield p. 5.

Cover photograph reproduced with permission of Tudor Photography.

Our thanks to Joanna Dring, Careers Co-ordinator, Banbury School, Oxon for her help in the preparation of this book.

Every effort has been made to contact copyright holders of any material reproduced in this book. Any omissions will be rectified in subsequent printings if notice is given to the Publisher.

Contents

Technical words, jargon and specialist terms are explained in the glossary.

The wide, wide world of IT

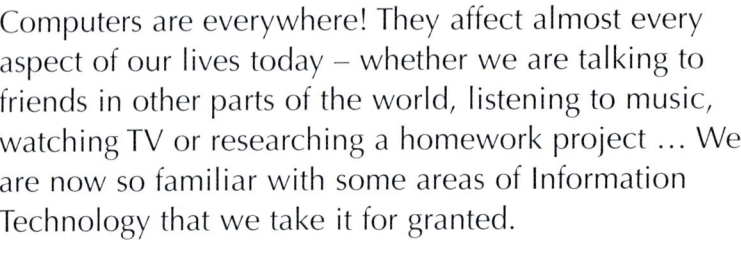

INFORMATION TECHNOLOGY

Computers are everywhere! They affect almost every aspect of our lives today – whether we are talking to friends in other parts of the world, listening to music, watching TV or researching a homework project … We are now so familiar with some areas of Information Technology that we take it for granted.

In recent years a revolution in communications, driven by the emergence of the personal computer and the Internet, has changed the way that business is conducted. We now live in a true Information Age, and we have seen the development of a genuine world-wide marketplace where there is an increasing range of products and services for sale along the superhighway.

Information Technology (or IT) is now the fastest growing part of the UK's economy. There are an estimated three quarters of a million people directly employed in IT at present, and this number looks set to grow.

IT can be an exciting field of employment and more and more people are considering it as a career choice – so let's find out what working in the wide, wide world of IT is really like!

Working in computers or using computers at work?

There is a real difference. It is almost impossible to think of any careers today that don't involve using computers, but for many of these jobs the main part of the work does not revolve around an understanding of the technology behind computers.

⭐ *This midwife is updating a patient's records straight on to the computer system while she is with her in the surgery.*

For many people, computers are the tools that enable them to work efficiently. For example, doctors and nurses working in general practice update their patients' personal records on computer while those patients are in the surgery, but this aspect of the job is only a tiny part of their work. Their main responsibility is of course to try to identify and ease any medical problems that their patients bring to them. Therefore you would say that a doctor uses a computer at work but does not work in computing.

But it is someone's job to develop the specialist computer program designed for use in medical practice. Someone maintains the computers. Someone devised the training manual which the doctor can refer to when needed. Someone sold the system to the doctor ... And so it goes on.

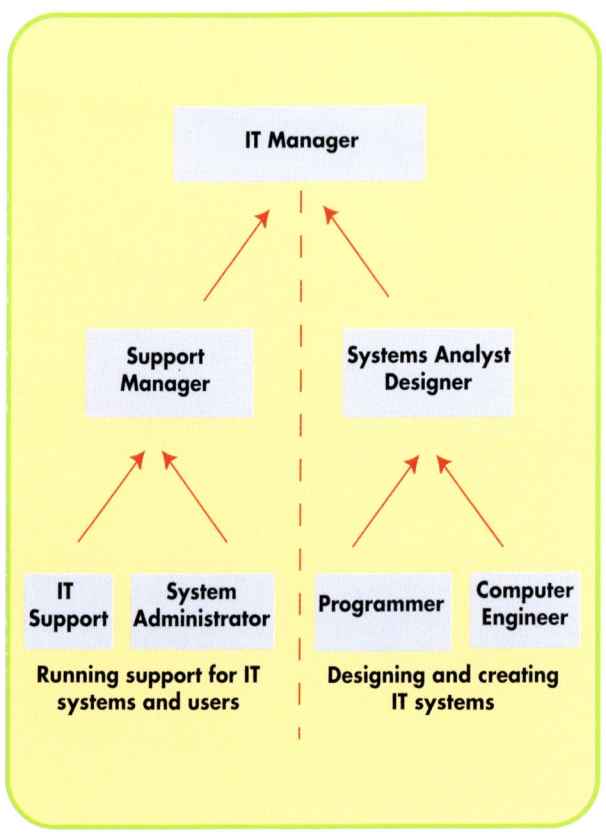

For many people, computers have become the 'tools of the trade' for the 21st century. There have always been toolmakers and menders, but the most useful and productive aspect of any tool is the work that you can do with it. The same can be said of computers. Most people who work with computers are not involved with the construction, or even the maintenance, of computers, although there are jobs in these areas, which this book will touch on. Most jobs in Information Technology have grown up around the millions of uses to which computers can be applied.

⭐ *This chart shows some of the inter-connection between jobs within IT.*

In this book we look at the main areas of employment directly involving Information Technology. You should never forget that computers have an impact on almost every aspect of our everyday lives. They also affect thousands of workers, from travel agents to talk show hosts.

One thing that becomes obvious as you get more familiar with the range of jobs in IT is that there is an enormous overlap between many different job areas. You can find programmers who are in charge of systems, analysts who program, support engineers who offer analysis. In such a large and developing industry there is such a huge range of jobs that opportunities exist for both the generalist and the specialist to find the area that suits them best.

All modern businesses now use Information Technology to support a wide range of day-to-day activities, from internal and external communications – e-mail and the Internet – through to financial management and forecasting. Many businesses include areas like project planning, development and sales in their IT. Using IT to manage information means that businesses can truly work world-wide. The Information Revolution that we are living through means businesses that were once restricted to dealing slowly by letter with clients and competitors can now contact them instantly across the globe. This has opened up all kinds of new opportunities, from dealing on the stock exchange to buying and selling at all levels through the Internet. The increasing availability of video conferencing and e-mail is affecting everyday business dealings throughout the world.

The range of jobs in Information Technology is huge and growing every day. As new applications are found to be posing new problems, so new jobs are created.
The aim of this book is to introduce and outline the key areas of IT and some of the employment opportunities that are available within the industry.

Video conferencing over the Internet enables people to have face-to-face meetings with others who are thousands of miles away.

Programmers

What is programming? The job of the **programmer** is to 'translate' what it is that you want the computer to do into a suitable form for the computer to read and act on. The programmer writes instructions in a form that the computer can understand by using a variety of computer languages. This is called writing 'computer software'.

Although there is a great deal more to working in computers than just programming, programming is an essential part of the field of Information Technology. The different problems that call for IT solutions require different programming languages. Programmers spend a lot of their time designing programs to suit specific situations.

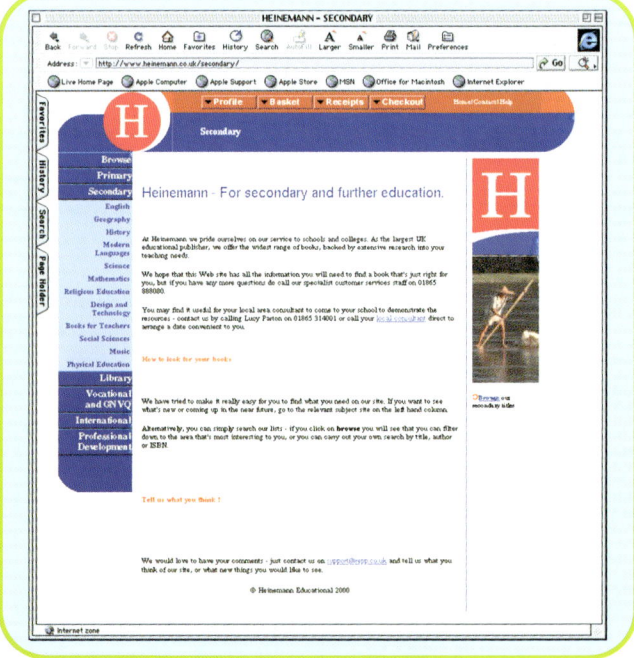

⭐ *Web page design and specific interactive Internet work are specialist areas for some programmers.*

CONSIDER THIS...

Programmers who enjoy the team-work aspects of the job could consider moving on to systems analysis or design work, but it is possible to stay as a specialist programmer. Many such highly skilled people earn extremely good salaries and are much sought after in the IT world.

Writing programs is a highly methodical and painstaking task. Every step that needs to be taken by a computer to complete a task accurately has to be written into the program. Designing and developing software from beginning to end is also an extremremely creative job and can be very satisfying.

There are a number of computer languages used in programming, and programmers therefore need to know these languages. Programmers often specialize in particular areas so that they can apply their skills to suit the specific needs of a computer user. Specialist areas include scientific applications, business applications, educational packages and games design. There are also programmers who specialize in web page design and interactive programs, and other work specific to the Internet.

Most programmers tend to specialize in one or two particular areas and need to know the computer languages that are applied in these areas. It is often necessary for programmers to learn new computer languages as they develop their careers and move into new areas. The languages themselves sometimes change to adapt to new applications. Programmers must keep up-to-date on all new developments in their area.

Programmers mostly work in teams under a project manager and they need to be able to communicate well with all members of the team and with the client. It is the client after all who commissions the work and pays the bill.

Is programming all the same?

There are at present two main areas of programming: applications and systems programming.

Applications programmers deal with information from outside the computer, for example word processing and the Internet.

Systems programmers develop programs that control the actual internal operation of computers. Systems programmers are often involved in writing diagnostic programs that can identify certain faults within the computer. They are also the people who write programs to control the running of several different programs at the same time.

Colin — Analyst Programmer

Colin Davidson works as a programmer for a large software consultancy. His job involves writing programs in two different computer languages (C++ and Visual Basic) for use in controlling production machinery in factories that manufacture cars. He works with two different development teams which include a number of other programmers.

My job is to write programs for the 'user interface' – what the machine operator sees on the computer screen. I have my own PC, which is networked to the rest of the company. Each morning I log on and download what I have been working on and spend most of the day at my screen. Every now and then there are team meetings to review the work. And two days a month I go out to the factory to see how my software might actually work in place.

Programmers like me earn around £20K per year and because I have to travel in my job I get a company car. You have to be persistent in this job because things very rarely work right first time. So when it doesn't work first time, you have to try, try, try again!

This is my second job since leaving university. I did a degree in Mechanical Engineering and that involved a project on Plant Automation. When I realized that I was enjoying the software side of that work more than the mechanical stuff I decided to get into software development through programming.

After university I joined a large software house as a graduate trainee programmer and stayed for four years learning all the basic programming skills. I moved to this job because it gave me the chance to specialize in the areas that I feel I am best at. With my background in Mechanical Engineering I have a good understanding of the customer's problems.

I like the challenge of the job – it's down to me to make things work! But there is a lot of pressure at times as some of the deadlines can be pretty tight.

⭐ *In the picture on the left, computer displays show the operator of automated equipment what is going on. These 'user interfaces' are written by specialist programmers, like Colin.*

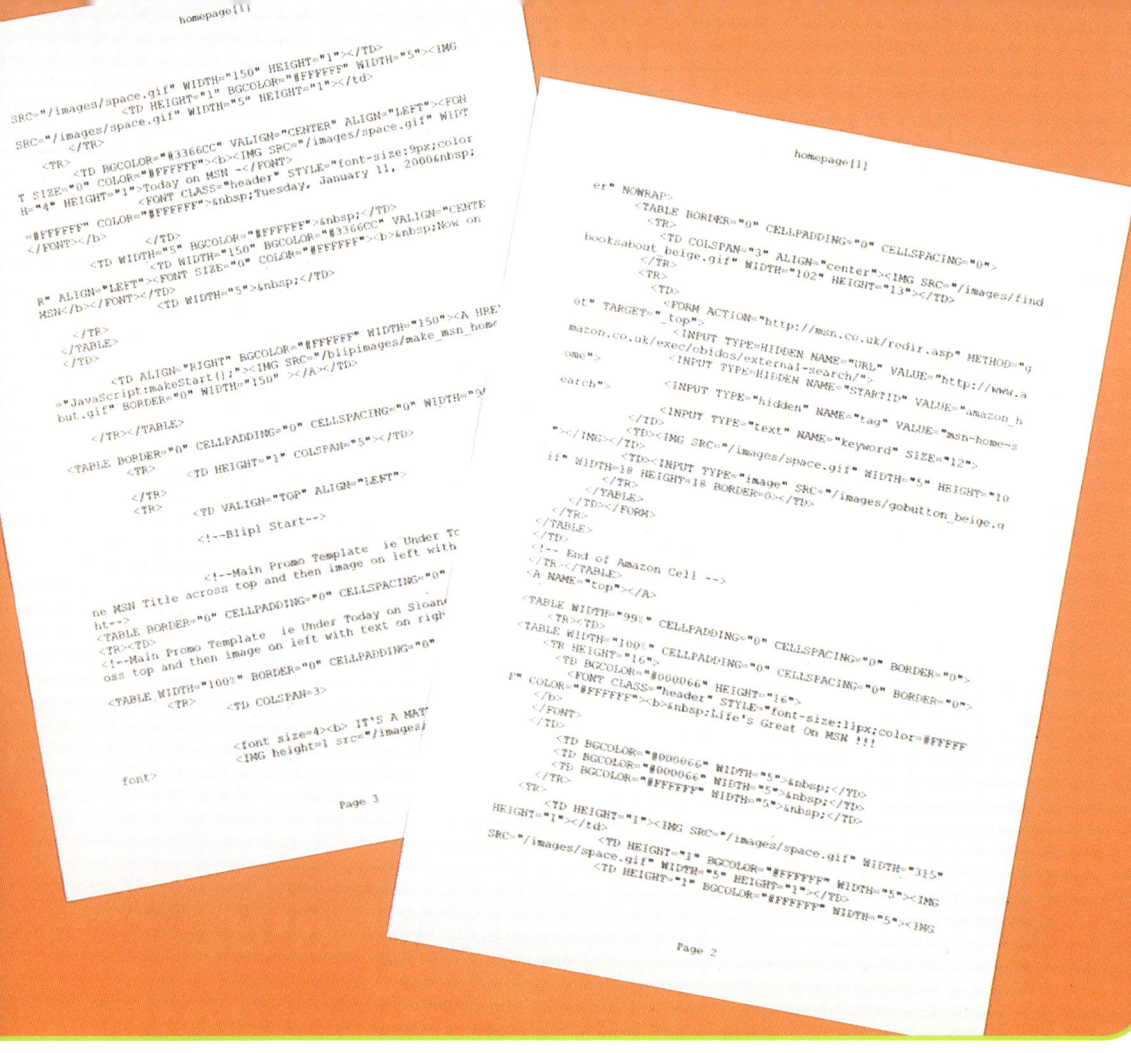

⭐ *Computer languages are a code of instructions to the computer enabling it to perform a task.*

It is quite a common practice for programmers to work on contract from one company to another. This can mean that they have to be very flexible about where they are based and be prepared to travel. Contract programmers tend to earn more money but also tend to have less job security. There are possibilities for experienced programmers to become self-employed, but part-time work is unusual. Because of the international nature of the IT industry there are lots of opportunities for experienced programmers to travel and work, especially if they speak a foreign language.

Systems analysts

Systems analysts design the computer systems that deal with a particular requirement. It is their job to say how the system should work and then make sure that it does.

A customer comes along with a particular problem looking for an IT solution. It is the analyst's job to investigate the needs of the customer so that they fully understand the background to the problem. They have to find out what the customer wants to achieve, if and how it can be done, and what effects there might be on the company's operations.

The implementation of a new system may well have effects on the customer's computer hardware needs and on other areas like staff training. The systems analysts have to make the customer aware of these implications. It is up to other IT staff to follow up on any identified needs.

When they have a full understanding of what is needed, the analysts can apply their knowledge of Information Technology to begin to design a system. This is usually done by drawing up a plan of what could be possible. When designing a system, analysts have to take into account issues that have a bearing on matters like finance, time scales and security as well as the technical aspects of the work. Analysts also have to consider any existing software systems that may already be in place and how the new system will fit with them. The plan that they design has to explain to the customer how the IT system will work, and all the implications that a new system may have for that customer.

Analysts who are employed by a large company may work on one main site but others working for consultancies may need to travel to the customer's base, which can involve a number of visits, each for some length of time. It is important to build up a good relationship with the client and the staff who will be working directly with the system, in order to establish a workable solution for that client's particular needs.

⭐ *The client explains to the systems analyst analyst exactly what she needs so that he can design the new IT system correctly.*

Systems analysts/designers need to have knowledge of all sorts of IT techniques and a high standard of report writing, since much of the information that they deal with has to be explained and passed on to other users in a clear, concise, and easily understood way. They have to take into account that some users may not be as computer literate as others.

Much of the information that an analyst may have to deal with may be of a specific technical nature, so it helps to have the ability to understand technical processes quickly. It is also useful to be able to work in detail and enjoy precise logical working whilst being able to take a broad view on what the customer may need. An analyst must be able to communicate well.

Many analysts also work as team leaders and **project managers** leading a group of **programmers**. This means that they also need to have management skills to get the best work out of their team.

Traditionally systems analysts have a background of working for two or three years in programming, although there are some companies that recruit graduates direct as trainee analysts.

Analysts, above all, need to be able to understand their client's point of view and have the flexibility to reach a solution that suits the problem. They have to have a realistic attitude to problem solving and enjoy the challenge of producing solutions using IT.

Systems analysts tend to work full-time for their employers; it is not as common for them to work on contract as it is for programmers. There is limited opportunity for part-time work at present.

This flowchart shows the working relationships within a typical IT project.

Customer has a problem and is looking for an IT solution.

↓

Systems analyst finds out what the customer needs, suggests an IT solution and explains repercussions.

↓

Project manager works with the analyst and team to supply a solution through systems design.

↓

Programmer designs programs for the system.

↓

Hardware engineer assesses the suitability of, and needs for, equipment and works on the installation.

↓

Support engineer supplies back-up support on equipment and on areas like training.

↓

Systems administrator looks after the smooth running of the installation once it is in place.

Diana – Systems Analyst

Diana Saunders works as a Lead Developer for a small software company that produces software for the water and gas industry.

It is my job to make sure that the computer software that our company produces is finished on time and does what it is supposed to do. I decide who does what in my team and how detailed their instructions have to be. I also write some of the software myself.

Day-to-day this means that I spend a lot of time sending and receiving e-mail messages instructing people in what to do and answering any queries they may have. Every hour or so, I walk around the offices checking up on progress. In between I try to get on with bits of software myself but it is hard to concentrate on this because of all the other stuff to do. You really need to have the ability to keep track of lots of things at once. You also need good management skills. It helps to be able to cajole people into doing things they don't always want to!

I have a degree in Maths during which I got to 'play' with some software, and have had a couple of similar jobs in the past. As I've changed jobs, I've tended to take on more responsibility. I get paid over £30K per year at the moment and have a company car.

I enjoy it when things go well – you get a real sense of achievement – but there are times when managing the team can be difficult and gets in the way of getting the work done.

⭐ *A systems analyst needs good communication skills to support and encourage the team working on her project.*

Systems administrators

The job of a **systems administrator** is to provide both the support and the organization for a particular computer system. (A computer system is a combination of computers linked together for a particular purpose.) The administrator oversees both the system itself and the software which is running on it.

The systems administrators operate the system and are sometimes called computer operators. Usually the system is in place to do a particular job. Perhaps it is set up in a school to deal with educational matters or in a business to deal with accounts.

⭐ *These computers are all linked together to form a system which is managed by a systems administrator.*

Computer systems, like computer languages, all have different names. You may be familiar with some already. Windows™ is an operating system that is used throughout the world. Operating systems, like computer languages, are designed for specific purposes. Administrators often have to be able to deal with a range of operating systems.

Administration can involve both hardware and software elements of computing. The job involves the repair, maintenance and updating of equipment and all the aspects of the software of a system ensuring security, suitability of program and even elements of training.

What is the difference between software and hardware?

Computer software is a term that covers the form of instructions that allows the computer to perform a task. Software can come in all sorts of specializations and is written by **programmers**. There is a growing number of specialist software packages that have been designed to deal with particular problems. For example, one specialist area is writing software packages used in education.

Computer hardware is a term that covers all of the equipment that is essential for computers to work. This includes everything from the computers themselves to the screens, modems, printers, scanners, leads and every other device that enhances the use of IT in the 21st century.

Seema – Systems Administrator

Seema Ali works for a large research company. It is her job to administer a large network of around 300 computers, which run a particular operating system called Unix.

Day-to-day this means the monitoring of the computer system and updating it as necessary. My job involves managing the use of the system and dealing with both the computer-related problems and those of the users themselves! I also have to take care of all the other devices attached to the computers – the printers, tape drives and the power supply. When new software or hardware is introduced I have to evaluate it to make sure that it all works as it should.

There is an element of troubleshooting in the job as I have to try to diagnose the fault and repair the system when there are problems. This often means isolating the specific problem to allow the rest of the system to operate. I did get training through the company in the operating system itself and in supporting the users.

You definitely need to be able to keep a cool head when things get stressful, but I do enjoy the challenge and variety of the job! This job pays over £20K per year; some people in similar jobs earn more.

I came into the job after a career change. I began to use computers when working in the Health Service and decided that there were opportunities in IT that interested me. I took a part-time HNC in Computing and then got this job.

⭐ Systems administrator Seema's work involves supporting the users as well as resolving problems with the system.

Duncan – Systems Administrator/ Information Specialist

Duncan Thomas works for a training company as part of their Business Systems Team and is responsible for the management of information through the computer system.

The main part of my job is to provide accurate information to the staff of the company and the Government Office that funds it, although I also work as part of the team that supports the whole computer system.

For one week every month I collect and prepare information on what work has been conducted within the company and present it to the management team in a form that they can easily understand. This involves 'translating' statistical material into a written report. This information is part of our contract with the Government and is used to monitor our work and plan any future developments – so it is vital to the company. It is my responsibility that this is delivered on time and that it is accurate.

I was working in another department in the company and transferred to this job nearly three years ago after deciding to move into IT-related work. I earn around £19K a year and all my training has been 'on the job'.

I like the fact that I know what is expected of me and can plan around certain things happening within the job every month. I am the sort of person who feels happy knowing what is expected of me. I am good at accurate work and I enjoy it.

What makes a good systems administrator?
To be a successful systems administrator, you need to be well organized and enjoy working with people. You need to have an expert knowledge of all the hardware and software elements of the computer system you are in charge of.

It would be wrong to give the impression that all work in IT requires people always to be dynamic. As with all industries there is such a wide variety of jobs: some pressured and full of change, others more routine and less unpredictable.

Systems administration includes elements of support, computer engineering, training and systems development and programming.

The opportunities for self-employment and part-time working are perhaps less than in other IT jobs because of the intense knowledge needed for a particular system and the importance of efficient, full-time administration. Administering the system can at times be as much about sorting out the users as the computers!

Some organizations 'contract out' their systems administration to specialist IT suppliers.

In some companies the system has to be kept going 24 hours a day so shift work may be necessary for the systems administrators. This can also apply to those working in IT support where it is often important that there is around the clock access to some IT systems.

Working in IT support

As more and more organizations make use of Information Technology, there follows a growing role for people who can train and support those using new systems and applications. **Support staff** may take it in turns to man 'help desks', where systems users can phone in with their IT queries. Another aspect of the support role might be the writing of help manuals to explain different procedures and remind staff about aspects of the training, for example the working of a new e-mail system.

⭐ *Help desk staff have a vital support role for users of the computer system.*

To be successful in IT support you must obviously have an understanding of the technology, but more importantly you must be able to communicate this understanding to other people. To be good at IT support you need to enjoy, and be skilled at, dealing with all sorts of different people with varying levels of understanding of and interest in IT. You also need to have a good understanding of the organization that you are working for and its needs. It also helps to have an interest in new IT developments.

IT training is one of the biggest growth areas there has been over the last few years. As computers have become more common in the work-place the need has developed to show people how best to use them. Whether offering training to individuals within a company or at evening classes, it is often the trainer's ability to pass on what they know that is more important than the expertise they have themselves. So, people involved in IT training not only need background knowledge of computing, but they also need to have an extremely good ability to communicate. Some trainers may undertake training themselves in teaching skills to back up their IT skills, and make them more effective in their jobs.

When a company introduces the Internet into their organization or updates an existing software system, all the workers have to be instructed in the use and usefulness of what is perhaps a totally new technology to them. Patience is needed to take people from the basic task of logging on and remembering passwords through to loading up software and making use of applications.

⭐ *IT training is a major growth area in business and commerce as well as in education.*

Barbara – IT Support

Barbara McCloud works as part of the support team at a University Computer Centre as a Computer Adviser.

To be good at this sort of work you have to be able to get on with all sorts of different people, ranging from students from all sorts of backgrounds and nationalities to lecturers and admin staff. You need to have patience and be a good communicator but also be able to work under pressure at times as everybody expects an answer to their particular questions straight away.

I work very much as part of the Support Team.

This is my first job after completing my HND in Computing. Before that, straight after GCSEs I did a BTec Diploma in Business Studies and worked for a number of different companies doing a range of office and administration jobs.

I particularly enjoy the contact that this job gives me with all sorts of different people. It can be very satisfying to help someone gain skills in IT. It's also great when you can sort out problems!

⭐ *University students welcome help from support staff like Barbara, to enable them to use the Computer Centre to their best advantage.*

Anthony – Support Engineer

Anthony Blackwell works for a company that develops and sells specialist software.

Basically my job is to provide technical support for all the products that we sell. This also involves training customers in how to make best use of our products. Day-to-day this means that I sit in front of a computer answering phones and sorting out any problems customers may have come across usually by suggesting possible ways that they may have 'got it wrong'. This can involve taking people right back to basics, as different customers have very different levels of IT experience. Post-sales support is very important to the company. The support must be accessible and efficient and it is up to us to make sure that the customer is kept happy and will use our company again in the future.

It helps to be good at communicating with people and to catch on to things pretty quickly. I have to deal with all sorts of people and problems and some of them can get pretty stressed, so it's good to be able to keep your cool.

I came into the job after doing a degree in Civil Engineering, not the standard route perhaps but I enjoyed working with computers at university.

All my training for the job has been 'on the job' with the odd training session thrown in! Support Engineers like me get around £16–18K per year but it varies according to the business you are in.

Likes? Well, working with nice people and the variety of work. And sometimes I get the chance to travel with the Sales team here and in the USA showing customers what the system can do.

Dislikes? Some customers can be impatient and want answers NOW! The work can be frustrating as it's difficult to get stuck into something without being constantly interrupted.

Working in IT management

We have all heard of people described as managers. But what does that mean? And what does it mean in IT? A manager is someone whose job it is to organize something or someone. In the world of computing that can mean organizing computer systems or people, but it usually means a bit of both.

All IT needs to be managed. Even a personal computer with only one user needs to be managed. Files need to be correctly stored, software loaded, equipment checked and serviced.

IT management exists at all levels. A school, a small office or shop, or a company with perhaps hundreds of staff all with their own computer terminals – they all have management needs. Someone has to be there to maintain the computer system that exists, and to help develop new systems for new problems and organize support for the people using the systems. We have looked at support staff and designers such as **systems analysts**. It is the IT manager who pulls together much of their work within an organization.

Adam – IT Manager

Adam Morgan works as an IT manager for a large commercial company with over 250 staff spread across the south east of England. Adam runs a small team of support staff and is based at the company's head office, but spends a lot of time travelling from site to site overseeing the installation of new equipment – hardware and software – as well as trouble-shooting any problems that staff may have with training or the running of the computer system. He decides what new equipment is needed, and he also works with his team on designing user guides and training manuals for other staff.

I moved into IT management after working as a Computer Consultant with a smaller company. That was my first job after doing a degree in Physics. I chose to move into computing after university because of the job opportunities and because I thought I'd be good at it!

I enjoy the fact that in this job I get to organize my own workload and take responsibility for what I do – even though there always seems to be more work than time so it can be pretty pressured. At the moment I am earning £25K per year plus a share in the company bonus scheme.

I'm not so keen on the amount of travelling that I have to do between sites. Also if there's a really big problem it's down to my team to fix it, otherwise the company just couldn't function, so at times we all have to work very long hours.

It helps to be a fairly logical person who can prioritize what needs to be done without getting too panic-stricken as people can get very stressed when things go wrong. I have to deal with all the members of the company including at times the company's chairman, so it is important that I keep calm under pressure and can communicate well with all sorts of different people!

⭐ *An IT manager like Adam needs to be a good organizer and be able to communicate easily with all his staff.*

Project management

This is an area of IT management that involves the responsibility for developing and implementing a particular contract. In many organizations it is often the introduction to a management role.

One look through the computing press, either through the Internet, magazines like *Computer Weekly* or the IT recruitment pages of national newspapers, will give you an idea of some of the opportunities that are available in **project management**. There are all sorts of different organizations offering a wide range of IT management jobs that include travel, company car schemes, and big wages for those with the right career background, the right range of skills and the right level of experience.

IT management combines many of the skills used in many of the other IT roles and is often the career aim for people in other IT jobs, with high salaries being offered by many companies. But no matter how good a programmer or analyst you might be, it is your skills in the management of your work load and in the management of people that will make you a success at this level.

Many IT projects follow a similar pattern and so it is useful to look at a typical 'life cycle' of a project to see the way that the various jobs interact. The example on the next page shows a major project involving a number of different partners.

A typical 'job' from customer approach through to delivery as seen by the project manager

Once upon a time ...

A computing consultancy is approached by an engineering company that works for the Indian government. It is looking at producing a cyclone warning system to predict the ever-increasing threat of cyclones in that part of the world. It is hoping for an IT solution. It becomes the customer.

... there was ...

A project manager works with systems analysts and programmers and their partner company to work out what an IT system could offer. They produce a plan including price and time-scale, which is accepted.

... a problem.

The team works together on producing a system – programmers write, systems designers design and the project manager and analysts consult with their customer. Documents are written outlining the system. There are trips to India for liaison with local IT and cyclone specialists. User documents are written. The system is tested and retested both on-site and in the office. Problems arise and are sorted out by the team.

An answer was found ...

Software and hardware are installed in India. Installation engineers are brought into the team as they are needed. The system is once again tested and then accepted by the customer.

... and they lived happily ever after.

Although accepted, there is still work to be done training staff on-site and supporting the software through any future problems. A maintenance contract is agreed and the relationship with the customer continues.

Working in IT sales

Work in **IT sales** could mean selling the hardware: the computers themselves and the back-up equipment like printers, scanners and modems. It could mean selling the software: the systems that the computer uses to carry out applications. Or it could mean selling personal computers and software direct to the public rather than to businesses and organizations. All of these areas will usually include the sale of the support that is needed for systems and equipment.

Whatever area of IT sales you are in, the job will draw on a mixture of technical knowledge and the ability to sell. At one end of the IT sales scale there is the high street retailer selling PCs and software to the public, whilst at the other end of the scale are the companies that pay millions of pounds for new systems and equipment.

⭐ *To work in IT sales, as Catherine does, it helps to have a technical interest, but it is also about talking to and dealing with the public.*

Catherine – Sales Adviser

Catherine Lawley works for one of the High Street chains that sell computer equipment direct to the public. The company also handles other technical items like cameras, mobile phones and TV/audio equipment.

I joined the company straight from school after my GCSEs. I had been introduced to the company through my school work-experience scheme, which went well and led onto a Saturday job in my last year of school. So I really knew what I was letting myself in for!

I was thinking about staying on and doing an IT course at college as I have always been into computers. But when the store offered me the job, with the money (I get £9.5K a year at the moment and staff discount on goods) and the training, it looked the better option. The main part of my job is advising customers about the full range of goods that we offer and helping them choose what suits them best. And hopefully making a sale!

I really enjoy talking to people about what they are looking for.

It helps that I am interested in IT and enjoy using it myself. I don't think it's the sort of thing you could sell if you weren't interested.

I also have to help keep the shop looking good, which means I have to do some cleaning and tidying – not something I really enjoy! But we work as a team and I have to do my share.

The company sent me on a week's training at their head office shortly after I joined. We regularly have training sessions covering new lines and customer service. I am working towards my Modern Apprenticeship in Customer Service, which means quite a lot of work completing a portfolio, but my manager and the other staff are pretty helpful. I should complete my Modern Apprenticeship in about 18 months' time. Hopefully! Later on I might think about trying for the company's management scheme.

What do I like about the job? Well I think it's the mixture of knowing about computers and dealing with customers.

The down side? Well, there's the cleaning. And working on Saturdays can be annoying, especially if my mates are free. But we try to work on a rota so it's not every weekend. And being on my feet all day. It kills your feet!

Peter – Technical Sales Director

Peter Baker coordinates the UK-based sales team of an American computer company which sells its products all over the world.

Day-to-day, the job involves answering queries from past and potential customers, sometimes at very short notice, and visiting customers before sales to discuss their initial needs and after-sales requirements as part of the follow-up service.

Our clients are spread throughout Europe so this can mean a number of trips away, usually to France, Germany and Italy, most of which I enjoy – but I don't always get to say when I can travel, which can interfere with my personal life.

It is part of my job to train the rest of the sales team in any new products that the company have introduced. Team-work is vital, and as the team leader, it is important that the other members of the team feel they can bring any problems to me. It is also up to me to organize the work and motivate the team to sell our products. I have to be aware of all new technical developments and this means several trips to the headquarters in USA for my own product training.

To be good at this job you need to have good communication skills, especially when you are explaining technical details to people who may not have an IT background. You need to be extremely outgoing for this type of work. Selling doesn't suit everybody and I believe that you have to enjoy the work to be good at it. You need to have lots of self-confidence to push yourself and the company's products forwards. It helps to be a bit of a performer at times!

I came to my present position after working in various technical computing posts following a degree in Electrical Engineering. The job is relatively well paid – I am on £40K plus commission at the moment – and I enjoy organizing my own work, but at times the travel becomes tiring. There is always lots of pressure to deliver the sales. The company's future lies in selling its products. That can be quite a responsibility at times!

IT sales staff need to balance the need for up-to-date technical knowledge with the knowledge of their potential customers' needs. It is important in all aspects of sales that staff have excellent communication skills and are good team players.

As with other fast-expanding industries, sales and marketing are vitally important to the growth and development of Information Technology both in the business world and in high street retailing. Without the customer the product would probably not exist!

Selling is a skill in itself. A Technical Sales Director needs to combine a technical understanding with the ability to communicate with, and influence, the customer.

Design opportunities in IT

Another area of related IT employment links design with computing.

Increasingly **programmers** are working more closely with other trained professionals. To produce computer games, specialist programmers work with graphic designers, animators, video producers and sound engineers.

Other design work using the skills of CAD **(computer-aided design)** has been employed in a number of industries for some time to produce vivid three-dimensional images for a whole range of applications. CAD is particularly suited to jobs that involve showing cable and pipe-work layouts and also to the intricacies of printed circuit boards which have many applications.

CAM **(computer-aided manufacture)** is now also widespread. Computer-controlled machinery is employed in many forms of production from large car-making plants down to the manufacture of complex components for the IT industry itself.

The whole field of **robotics**, which follows on from the field of computer-controlled machinery, is an exciting aspect of IT. Artificial intelligence – the ability of a machine to perform functions similar to those of a human brain – is still in the early stages of development but is one to which a great deal of research is being applied. This may well provide new employment prospects in the near future.

Andy – CAD/CAM Project Manager

Andy Rivers works for one of the largest car manufacturers in the world. He leads a team of programmers and designers who work on design projects for the company. Andy's team uses CAD programs and computer simulations to test things like ride quality, handling and aerodynamics.

My job involves a lot of liaison with our engineers and car designers, and with my team. I did a degree in Computer Studies at university and specialized in computer-aided design. I have always been a practical person and enjoyed Design Technology at school. I wanted a job that would combine my practical ability with my interest in computers.

A lot of my time is spent 'managing' projects, which means that I have to be aware of how we are doing with the work – whether we are on schedule and in budget. As a manager I am paid £38K and have a company car.

Towards the end of a project the whole team tends to work late to get it in on time. But it comes down to be my responsibility in the end! I get to do some hands-on stuff occasionally and I help train any junior staff, which I enjoy.

⭐ *Computer-aided design (CAD) has applications in many fields, and helps designers like Andy resolve difficult aerodynamic problems.*

Computer engineering

Engineers in IT

Computer engineers need a strong technical understanding. It is often their role within a team of other practitioners to understand both how the hardware works and how it will fit together with the software.

Software engineers, sometimes called **software designers**, are employed in specialist roles to create and test software and the equipment that delivers software. They often work in manufacturing or scientific employment or are contracted to this type of work through software consultancies. They are highly valued because they have a knowledge of both software and hardware. Software engineers tend to work on what is called 'low level software' – the sort of program which is intelligible to the computer but not to the computer user. These are the programs that instruct the computer on what steps are needed to produce the necessary application.

Computer engineering is a relatively new term and there is some obvious overlap with some types of programming and some systems analysis/design.

CONSIDER THIS...

IF COMPUTER ENGINEERING/DESIGN OR COMPUTER MAINTENANCE ENGINEERING APPEALS TO YOU THEN YOU MIGHT LIKE TO CONSIDER OTHER FORMS OF ENGINEERING.
THESE ARE JUST SOME EXAMPLES:
* MECHANICAL
* ELECTRICAL/ELECTRONIC
* AERONAUTICAL
* PRODUCTION
* TELECOMMUNICATION.

CONSIDER THIS...

ONE DEFINITION OF COMPUTING COULD BE 'FINDING SOLUTIONS TO REAL PROBLEMS'. THIS DEFINITION CAN ALSO BE APPLIED TO ENGINEERING. IF YOU HAVE THOUGHT ABOUT ENGINEERING AS A CAREER WHY NOT TAKE A LOOK AT COMPUTER ENGINEERING?

There is also an overlap between other types of engineering – electronic, mechanical and control engineering – and computer engineering. Many projects involving computer technology need people who can make use of the technical aspects of their own engineering expertise and also have the IT skills needed to understand how and when to use such applications.

Penny - Software Engineer

Penny Tyler works for a large engineering company that produces navigation equipment for aircraft. Her job is to write and test the computer programs that make the navigation equipment work – telling the plane how high it is flying, where it is in the air and in which direction it is headed.

My programs have to calculate the speed and direction of the aircraft and send the information to the pilot's display. As well as writing the programs I have to test them, firstly using simulated data and testing the actual equipment on the bench. Then the fun starts and I have to do tests in the air! This usually involves flying along the cliff edge to get as much turbulence as possible to see how the stuff copes. You need a strong stomach for this job!

Actually it helps to have a real interest in technical things. I've always loved planes and enjoyed flying.

I did an Advanced GNVQ in Engineering and A level Maths after GCSEs and then a degree in Control Engineering before this job. I earn around £22K per year.

The job can be very hard work and we often work late as the customer always wants delivery yesterday, but I really enjoy the variety. It is important to work accurately and carefully in this job. I never let myself forget that I am designing something that must work. If the system were to fail people's lives could be at stake. It's important!

I get to do all aspects of the project because I am involved from the start of the project right through to delivery.

All part of a team ...

No matter what form of engineering you might be considering, whether mechanical, electrical or computer, one important element that is common to all engineers is the need to work as part of a team.

It is unusual for an engineer to work in isolation. Even when they are brought in to troubleshoot problems, engineers must be aware of the other roles involved in all the aspects of computer development and maintenance. They might be brought into a project or a problem at a later stage but they need to have knowledge and understanding of what has gone on before their arrival in order to effect a solution.

Engineers need to be logical thinkers who enjoy problem solving and, like the systems analyst, they must enjoy finding real solutions to real problems using their particular skills.

Testing systems and equipment is an important part of the computer engineer's job – in this case as part of a motor racing team.

Installation and maintenance

There are different levels of engineer working in the industry. **Maintenance and installation engineers** tend to be trained in their particular skills by others in the field, whereas those involved in other areas of computer engineering generally have gained relevant degrees before starting work.

This type of work employs a large number of people in a variety of functions within the IT industry. There are some common elements between them insofar as they all need to bring a combination of technical skills and the ability to deal with people to their job.

Installation and maintenance are usually 'out and about' jobs, where travelling from site to site takes up quite a large proportion of the working day.

Another aspect of the job that installation and maintenance engineers have in common is that they often work independently, perhaps covering their own patch. They tend to be solely responsible for the work that they do. As with the areas of IT support and systems administration, some of those employed in installation and maintenance engineering have to work shift patterns, maintaining computing facilities that need to be operational 24 hours a day.

Mel – Computer Maintenance Engineer

Mel Sampson works for a company that provides engineering support for automatic teller machines – the 'hole in the wall' cash machines at banks and buildings societies. He has his own 'patch', which covers most of the south west of England.

Our customers contact me directly by phone so that I only have to go into the office once a week. I have a company car and carry all the equipment I am likely to need with me.

A lot of the problems are fairly routine and I try to get as much information from the client on the phone as I can. Sometimes I can tell them how to fix it themselves. But most calls require a visit. I have to 'guess' how long each call might take. It's important to give our clients an idea of when I should be with them, but that can be the hardest part of the job to get right!

You have to be pretty confident and self-reliant in this job. And you need to be able to keep your cool as there's always too much work and not enough time to do it in. People can get quite impatient with you because often they have their own customers and bosses getting at them! If I get something that I can't deal with, I can phone the office to get help, but I've been doing the job for so long now that I think that I've just about seen everything.

My training with this company was on the job. I spent a month on the road with an experienced person showing me the ropes. Now I'm the one that they choose to train new people. That's great!

I always enjoyed tinkering with things when I was younger. I looked at other types of engineering but chose to do a BTec in Computing Studies because I thought there would be some good jobs in IT. I then worked for an electronic engineering company for a few years before going out on the road.

I like the fact that I organize my own workload in this job, but I cover a big area so I do spend a lot of time on the road, which can be frustrating.

Long term? Well I've been looking at self-employment – contracting work, which would mean more money. (I earn about £25K+ at present.) But then I'd have to handle the business side of things, buy my own car and things.

I'll see!

⭐ *The IT industry needs the back-up of a maintenance engineer like Mel to keep the customers happy.*

A look into the future

Opportunity knocks!

The total work-force of people involved in IT in the UK is estimated to be at least three-quarters of a million and shows every sign of growing! IT-related jobs account for more than 10% of all new jobs in the last three years.

At first computers were huge boxes that took up whole rooms and needed information fed into them on cards with holes in! Then they got smaller and smaller and smaller.

Then came laptops and the Internet. So …

What is next?

Research into the future developments of computers and their uses is big business in itself. Companies in this field spend enormous sums of money trying to 'second guess' where the next big development will come and those like Microsoft are looking at making computers easier to use for everybody. One big area of research is investigating how to move away from a keyboard-based computer to a more truly interactive computer: one that you can talk to and that will talk back!

Developments in IT and communications are evolving every day. Links between mobile phones and the Internet via computers make IT even more mobile and accessible. Our homes are becoming more and more computer-orientated with DVD playing through personal computers, newly released music tracks being issued on-line before they are available in the shops, and more. As we have seen in the past, where there are new developments in IT there are jobs.

Over the relatively short time (about forty years) that computers have been with us, many of the original jobs in IT have changed both in their content and their title. Changes are happening all the time and with increasing speed. Employers are always talking about the need to have people in the industry who are flexible and adaptable. These attributes are essential in many areas to keep pace with the speed of development and change.

Not long ago **web site design** was the newest job area to appear in the IT industry. You are probably familiar with the look of pages on the Internet. It is someone's job to design these pages, someone's job to develop the software that generates what you see on the screen. It might be one person, but it is more likely to be a team effort, perhaps employing graphic designers for the look and **programmers** for the software. There are still programmers who specialize in web site design, but the technology has moved on so quickly that a few years down the line, it is now possible to set up and design your own web page. The software is readily available.

Another new field of development is in **multi-media production**: multi-media meaning systems that combine aspects of text, data, graphics, sound and images to produce a virtual reality. This form of production is used increasingly in computer games, film, video at home and in work. **Computer games design**, **production**, **sales** and **marketing** are other examples of how the fast-developing IT industry can open up whole sections of employment that had previously not existed. **Virtual reality simulation** is used in the training of pilots and emergency personnel, for example, paramedics and fire fighters.

CONSIDER THIS...

THE IT INDUSTRY IS HEAVILY RELIANT UPON THE COMMUNICATIONS INDUSTRY. ADVANCES IN COMMUNICATIONS – PHONE LINES TRANSPORTING THE INTERNET, THE DEVELOPMENT OF THE MOBILE PHONE – HAVE GONE ALONGSIDE DEVELOPMENTS IN IT. MANY JOBS IN COMMUNICATIONS REQUIRE SIMILAR SKILLS AND BACKGROUND TO THOSE NEEDED IN IT. FOR EXAMPLE THE WORK OF A TELECOMMUNICATIONS ENGINEER CAN BE VERY SIMILAR TO THAT OF AN IT MAINTENANCE AND SUPPORT ENGINEER. THERE ARE ALSO OPPORTUNITIES FOR SYSTEMS ANALYSIS AND PROGRAMMING IN THE COMMUNICATIONS INDUSTRY.

The immersive technology of virtual reality (where the user can influence the progress of the three-dimensional program and interact with the software through using specialist hardware such as headsets) is becoming more and more important in the commercial world. Architects and product designers are just some of the people who are using the technology to sell their skills and their products to their customers before completion of any actual models.

The fields of multi-media and virtual reality simulation bring together people from all kinds of diverse backgrounds – musicians, sound engineers, graphic artists, video producers – but all of this technology is dependent on the development and implementation of new systems of software and hardware. And that is where the programmers, the systems designers and the computer engineers come in!

⭐ *Training pilots on realistic flight simulators is safer and saves time and resources.*

Training for a changing industry

Things move so quickly within the IT industry that you may ask, 'How do I know what to train for when the jobs themselves might have changed?' Although the changes that have already taken place within the industry have affected some working practices and certainly some job titles, there are many job skills that have remained unaffected by the changes.

What skills are needed?

- Communication skills
- Interest in technical matters
- Adaptability
- Enthusiasm for learning and training
- Flexibility.

There has been a revolution in the fields of information, communications and technology. Powerful computers have become smaller, cheaper and more portable. Now telephone lines carry e-mail messages thousands of miles. The situation is still changing and with the expected growth of remote access working – people working away from their main site, perhaps at home, linked to the office by phone line – there are growing opportunities for more flexible working, home working, part-time or contract work.

It has long been said that with the communication and IT revolution there would be a revolution in the way that people work. It was predicted by some that the traditional pattern of office- and business-based work would disappear and be replaced by home-based working with staff communicating only by remote access computer link by phone line.

With the Internet, and specifically e-mail, people can and do work away from the office, but as yet the revolution is still in the early stages. A lot of work still takes place in face-to-face meetings. Who knows, perhaps people just like to get together occasionally! Of the total IT work-force at present in the UK, 92% are employed full time and 8% employed part time; of those working full time, 7% are self-employed or IT contractors. But who can say what the future may hold?

With the growth of on-line shopping for an increasing range of goods and services, jobs are being created not only in the IT that supports Internet services but also in new areas of development in commerce and supply. So much business is now carried out through the Internet that some operations like the stock market have been revolutionized because of the speed and accessibility of what is now known as e-commerce. In recent years entrepreneurs have made millions of pounds through dealing in IT shares and buying and selling things like web sites.

You can be sure that there will be more and more jobs involving computers in the future.

The future is yours!

The IT industry is dynamic and going places! Jobs within IT are still developing and growing. Many employees are young and newly qualified. More and more computer-related degrees and FE courses are available every year. There are opportunities for both males and females to advance within the industry provided that they are enthusiastic about the work and are prepared to train and adapt in such a fast moving world.

Getting into IT

As shown by the people we have spoken to who are already working in IT, there are all sorts of ways that you can start working in the industry. You can find examples of people who came into the industry unskilled and who are self-taught, but as the IT industry itself and training and education in IT develop, this avenue of entry becomes less likely.

It is true in most areas of IT that gaining qualifications, through training or education, at the highest level that you can, is likely to open up more opportunities. Many of your decisions will depend on what you want to do next and to a certain extent on what type of job you are heading for. Whether you want to stay on in education after your GCSEs or whether you want to begin your training in employment – the decision has to be yours.

What GCSE subjects are best for IT careers?

An interest and ability in Maths and Physics is useful for some IT careers, and communication skills are important, so English is helpful. Some schools offer computing at GCSE level but if yours does not, don't panic! At GCSE level you should be aiming to achieve a good cross-section of subjects, choosing those that you enjoy as well as those that will be useful in your career. Employers and college and university tutors are not looking for you to specialize too much at GCSE; they are more interested in a 'good general standard of education'. So you get your GCSEs over and done with. Then ... what's next?

Here are the options:

- A vocational qualification in Further Education is a qualification that equips you to work in a particular employment field.

  General National Vocational Qualification (GNVQ) in Information Technology is offered at different levels depending on what GCSE grades you have, how long you want to study and what you are aiming for. The courses offer practical computer time and project work. Students are continually assessed and also study literacy and numeracy skills and probably undertake some relevant work experience.

  Advanced GNVQ can be taken as a full or single award depending on what else you want to study. They can both usually be taken with AS levels or A2 levels and can be accepted for entrance to most related University courses.

  BTec in Information Technology, again offered at different levels, is a similar qualification to the GNVQ with lots of practical computer time and project work. It lasts up to three years and can be taken full time or part time.

  Entry to BTec Diploma is normally with four or more GCSEs at grade C+ or equivalent. Again, grade work is assessed as you progress, with built-in work experience. BTec Diploma qualifications are accepted for University entrance in most related courses.

- You can continue studying more than one subject, either to spread your options because you are not committed to a particular employment area or because you want to continue certain subjects you enjoy on to a higher level.

Advanced levels (A levels and AS levels) are available in a whole range of different subjects including Computing and IT. It is important that you have achieved certain grades at GCSE to ensure success. You are likely to study for two years, taking up to five subjects to AS level at the end of the first year, then dropping to three or four subjects to follow up to the full A2 level. Remember you can mix and match A, AS and Advanced GNVQ full and single qualifications.

- You might be keen to get straight into employment and start your training after your GCSEs. You might want to work towards a Modern Apprenticeship or a National Traineeship. These are available throughout the country and offer work-related training as a way of getting started in IT whilst working in the industry.

National Vocational Qualifications (NVQs)
These are available in a range of IT subjects and at a number of different levels. You usually work for NVQs whilst you are being trained and paid by a relevant employer. Each qualification is an assessment of a number of tasks and skills that you have gained and that are directly related to your work. It is possible to enter related Higher Education courses with the right level of NVQs.

Higher National Diplomas (HND)/ Higher National Certificates (HNC) are offered in Information Technology subjects in many colleges and universities. There is a whole range of courses, including specialist qualifications like Business Information Systems. HNDs are normally studied over two years full time. HNCs are offered as equivalent part-time courses, usually over a longer period of time. Entry to HND/C is usually with BTec Diploma, Advanced GNVQ/NVQ Advanced qualifications or equivalents.

- **Degrees** in IT and related subjects are also widely available. Degree titles vary enormously: Computer Studies, Computer Science, Business Computing, Software Development, Information Systems. The content of degree courses will vary too, depending how specialized or wide-ranging the course is. It is always important for prospective students to study prospectuses carefully and, if possible, to visit the departments, to gain a full understanding of what they are applying for.

  IT degrees can be taken alongside other subjects in Joint Honours courses or in Modular Degrees where a number of subjects is covered.

  IT Sandwich Degrees, where a year is spent in a relevant industry, are also available. Some IT employers offer sponsorship for students following degree courses which might involve some work experience.

  Degrees usually last three or four years and can often be taken part time. Entry is usually with BTec Diploma, Advanced GNVQ and A levels or equivalent. Some degree courses are accredited by the British Computer Society and can exempt graduates from part of their professional examinations.

Employers recruit graduates with degrees in subjects other than IT for IT training. There are also 'conversion' courses available for people whose first degree is not directly IT-related to gain IT skills.

- **Professional qualifications** are offered through the British Computer Society for staff working in all parts of the IT industry. Part-time courses are taken through college or correspondence course.

  The Institute of Management Studies also offers professional qualifications.

Is IT for you? Some clues...

There are some common themes in the multitude of jobs in the IT industry.

To work in IT systems and engineering it helps to have a logical way of thinking and enjoy problem solving. If you enjoy and are good at Maths this might be for you. Many computing courses include Maths in their teaching. But don't be put off if you find higher level Maths too difficult.

Science, particularly Physics, is relevant to IT and computing engineering with its emphasis on analysis and problem solving.

The importance of having good communication skills is constantly stressed. School subjects like English Language and Literature, History, Geography and Humanities can all demonstrate an ability to communicate effectively.

If you enjoy the IT applications in Business Studies there are many courses and jobs in Business Computing and related fields.

Foreign Languages are very useful in this global industry and can be taken with many IT courses. They might indicate an interest in translating and working with IT languages as a programmer.

With Art and Design and Music there are increasing opportunities for creative people in multimedia IT. If you enjoy Design Technology then you might enjoy engineering support or design.

And then of course there is ICT (Information, Communication and Technology) or Computing itself!

Useful information,
addresses & contacts

If you are interested in a career in IT, or think you might be, there are many things that you can do to find out more.

You should be able to find lots of information in your school's careers library or the library of your local Careers Service.

You'll find IT information under CAV in the library catalogue.

Help yourself

Any opportunity that you get to talk to people actually working in the IT world, take it! You might not think that you know anyone working in IT, but the chances are that you do!

Does your school have a computer system? If so, there may be a Systems Administrator walking the school's corridors. And what about IT lessons? Ask your teacher about how they got into IT teaching. There may be some interesting stories to hear!

Find free demonstrations and tutorials in computer magazines or on the Intenet. Teach yourself as much as possible: learn by doing!

Is there a Computer Club in school?

If there is, get involved! If there isn't, try getting one started. It may give you some programming experience and you are likely to meet people with similar ideas. Remember, IT is about team working.

Work experience

If your school offers work experience, then ask about opportunities with local IT employers. You might not be able to learn how to be a programmer in one week, but there may well be things you can do and it will give you a real insight into the industry. Approach local companies and ask if you can do work experience in the holidays.

These organizations will each give you more information on IT and IT careers

The National Training Organization for Information Technology
16–18 Berners Street
London
W1P 3PP
Tel: 020 7580 6677
Fax: 020 7580 5577
e-mail aiss@itnto.org.uk
www.aiss.org.uk
www.itnto.org.uk

British Computer Society
1 Sanford Street
Swindon
SN1 1HJ
Tel: 01793 417417
www.bcs.org.uk
Publishes *Inside Careers –
IT Profession Careers Guide*

Computing Services and Software Association
Hanover House
73–74 High Holborn
London
WC1V 6LE
Tel: 020 7395 6700
www.cssa.co.uk

Electronics and Software Services
National Training Organization
Old Chambers
93–94 West Street
Farnham
Surrey
GU9 7EB
Tel: 01252 720843
www.ess.org.uk

Engineering Careers Information Service
Vector House
41 Clarendon Road
Watford
Herts
WD1 1HS
Tel: 0800 282167
www.emta.org.uk

The National Computing Centre Ltd
Oxford House
Oxford Road
Manchester
M1 7ED
Tel: 0161 228 633
www.ncc.co.uk

Institute of IT Training
Institute House
Sir William Lyons Road
University of Warwick Science Park
Coventry
CV4 7EZ
Tel: 024 7641 8128
www.iitt.org.co.uk

Institute of Management

2 Savoy Court
Strand,
London
WC2R OEZ
www.inst-mgt.org.uk

Institute for the Management of Information Systems

5 Kingfisher House
New Mill Road
Orpington
Kent
BR5 3QG
Tel: 020 8308 0747
www.imis.org.uk

British Interactive Multimedia Association

5–6 Clipstone Street
London
WIP 7EB
Tel: 020 7436 8250
www.bima.co.uk

Institute of Analysts and Programmers

Charles House
36 Culmington Road
London W13 9 NH
Tel: 020 8567 2118
www.iap.org.uk

Women in Computing

c/o Janet Stack
Computing Science Dept
Glasgow University
17 Lilybank Gardens
Glasgow G12 8RZ
osiris.sunderland.ac.uk/wic/

Useful publications

Guide to Careers in Computing and Information Systems, published by British Computer Society.

A Brief Guide to Information Technology and Systems, a free booklet published by NTO IT.

CONSIDER THIS...

SOME MAJOR EMPLOYERS HAVE THEIR OWN WEB SITES OUTLINING THE SORT OF JOB OPPORTUNITIES THEY OFFER, FOR EXAMPLE WWW.BBC.CO.UK/JOBS HAVE A LOOK AT THEIR IT DEPARTMENTS TO SEE WHAT THEY DO.

Working in Information Technology, published by COIC (Central Office for Information on Careers).

Careers in Computing and Information Technology, published by Kogan Page.

Occupations, published by COIC.

Information Technology Casebook, published by Hobsons. This gives details of post-graduate courses and is a useful insight into graduate employment.

Information Technology published by Graduate Careers Advisory Service (GCAS). Introduction to the industry and jobs within IT, aimed at new graduates and those considering higher education.

Computer Science Courses 2000 published by UCAS/Trotman. Useful for information on wide range of HE courses available and the differences between them.

Degree Course Guide in Computer Science, published by CRAC (Careers Research and Advisory Centre).

Courses for Careers in IT published by Hobsons with the HESA (Higher Education Statistics Agency). Gives some useful background information on HE courses and graduate employment in industry.

IT NOW and Prospects Focus on IT. Both industry publications aimed at newly qualified graduates with advertised jobs and articles.

Handbook of Information Technology, published annually by CRAC/Hobsons Press. This describes a variety of graduate IT jobs and training opportunities.

For information on job prospects and availability within the IT industry, try accessing one of the on-line appointment pages like Computer Appointments at www.it-opportunities.co.uk or look in *Computer Weekly* or other computer magazines which are full of adverts and articles.

Newspapers often have useful articles and information. *The Guardian* and *The Times* regularly feature IT supplements each Thursday.

To find out about NVQs, National Traineeships and Modern Apprenticeships, ask your Careers Adviser or Careers Teacher for opportunities in your local area.

Get the jargon – a glossary of IT terms

applications programmer person who deals with information from outside the computer itself

artificial intelligence (AI) the area of IT aiming to reproduce the workings of the human brain, often involving speech patterns, information processing and game playing

CAD (computer-aided design) programs that enable users to 'draw' on the screen, giving realistic three-dimensional images

CAM (computer-aided manufacture) programmed machinery often in a factory setting that performs set tasks controlled by computer

computer languages instructions which computers 'understand'. Different languages have different names and are used for particular purposes

computer literate someone who is computer literate is confident about using a computer

computer system a number of computers linked together for a particular purpose

contract work someone who does contract work is employed for a particular project or projects rather than in a permanent job

diagnostic program means of identifying certain faults within a computer

download to call up information on computer

e-mail a method of contact through the Internet

end user someone who ultimately gets to work the computer or computer program

graduate person who has passed a degree

global marketplace the ability for businesses to buy and sell through computer technology linking individuals around the world

hardware the 'machinery' of computing including printers, monitors, etc

Information Age because of the revolution in communications, the period we live in is often referred to as this, rather like the Industrial Age, which came before

interactive relationship between computer and user which allows information to flow between the computer and the user

multimedia the working together through IT of sound, music, video, animation and graphics

laptop a small portable PC that can be operated away from a power source

log on to open up a computer, often with a personal password

network sends information between computers within a connected system

operating system the software that makes a computer perform tasks

PC, personal computer a small-scale unit which is portable and can be used almost anywhere

plant automation factory equipment which is operated by computer-controlled machines

portfolio file of evidence built up in work or education to show learning and progress

program the instructions that cause a computer to perform certain tasks

programmer person who writes and designs programs

remote access working on computer away from main site linked by phone lines

security an important aspect of computing where information often needs to be protected from other users

software anything to do with the instructions that tell a computer what to do

software consultancy company that concentrates on working on computing projects

specification the plan that outlines all aspects of a particular job

sponsorship a financial award, for example from a company to a student

superhighway the communications system, the Internet, which makes it possible for people around the world to have contact through their computers

systems analyst someone who works out and designs a computer system to solve a client's particular IT problem

systems programmer someone whose job is to work on information that controls the internal operation of a computer

user interface what the person using the computer sees on the screen

virtual reality the creation, by computer, of a life-like world on the screen with which the user can interact

Index